A VIOLINIST'S GUIDE

FOR

EXQUISITE INTONATION

BARRY ROSS

Printed in the United States of America by Tichenor Publishing Group, a division of T.I.S., Inc.

Copyright © 1989 by the American String Teachers Association.
All Rights Reserved

ISBN 0-89917-520-1

CONTENTS

PREFACE

I first became fascinated with the question of violin intonation while studying with Professor Broadus Erle at the Yale School of Music in 1968. Mr. Erle introduced me to the importance of sympathetic vibrations and combination tones in my studies of the *Bach Sonatas and Partitas*. He encouraged me to pursue these questions further, and suggested that a full study of violin intonation would be of great value to stringed instrument pedagogy. With Mr. Erle's encouragement, I delved into a study of violin intonation.

Over the years certain truths about intonation began to appear to me. During a sailing trip in 1984, surrounded by peace and natural beauty, I discovered the existence of the sympathetic touch tones. My discovery seemed to prove the theories which I had already formulated. And it provided an important starting point for this book.

The sympathetic touch tones prove that it **is** possible to determine exactly when a note is in tune and to duplicate that particular tuning at will. This is the level, surprisingly, at which many students and professionals encounter intonation as a problem. They are not sure whether a note is in tune.

If you are able to **decide upon** and **hear** the proper tuning, then you can always be sure to play it. What is most necessary is that you take the time to **search out** the ideal tuning and question the pitches to which you have become accustomed.

It is my hope that this book will provide concepts and exercises that will assist advanced players to substantially improve their intonation and thereby increase the beauty and expressiveness of their playing.

ACKNOWLEDGMENTS

The preparation of this book was greatly assisted by a number of dedicated friends. For his early encouragement and editorial advice I wish to thank Dr. Gerald Fischbach, past president of the Americation String Teachers Association. Daniel Heifetz, Syoko Aki Erle, and Diane Crandall all offered excellent suggestions as the book progressed. I am grateful to the faculty and administration of Kalamazoo College for providing leave time to develop this project, and to a very remarkable man named Irving Gilmore and the Irving Gilmore Foundation for helping to make this work possible.

I especially want to thank Jane Ross for her support, encouragement, and assistance during the years in which this project has evolved, and Robert Klotman of the American String Teachers Association for assisting with the publication.

FOR

MIRIAM

Drawings of Great String Players
by
Rhoda Ross
and Victoria Littna

INTRODUCTION

In order to play a note *exquisitely* in tune, one must <u>search out</u> the correct or preferred pitch among a variety of possible tunings. In fact, the word "exquisite" derives from the Latin *exquirere*, meaning **to search out, to select carefully, to choose.**

Traditionally, the process of developing beautiful intonation has involved rather subjective and incomplete criteria for determining ideal pitches for a given passage. Some players strive for "a good average" of in-tune-ness while others look for ways to make notes "feel" in tune. The semantic confusion alone is overwhelming. We hear of tempered tuning, just tuning, leading tone tuning, Baroque tuning, Pythagorean tuning, expressive tuning, piano tuning, string quartet tuning, all of which add to the confusion of an already muddled issue. My purpose is to provide a systematized approach that will help the devoted string player explore intonation and make decisions based upon the musical context and the perfect tuning of the instrument.

Even advanced players often do not understand that **tones which function differently must be played at different pitches.** The first finger *e* on the D string can at once be in tune with the open G and out of tune with the open A. This leads to the conclusion that there must be more than one possible tuning for certain notes. The question is, "How do you know when to make a note higher and when to make it lower?" Most answers to this question have been, until now, entirely subjective.

This book will present two types of tuning: MELODIC and HARMONIC. It will give students and professionals a solid basis for determining the proper intonation for almost every pitch. By practicing the SYMPATHETIC VIBRATIONS, MELODIC SCALES, HARMONIC SCALES, COMBINATION TONES, ORIGINAL ETUDES, and EXCERPTS contained in this book, the advanced player will have a means by which to examine intonation, adjust it in terms of its musical context, relate it to the open strings of the instrument, and explore a variety of tuning possibilities in the process of determining the most perfect tuning for each note.

Ten minutes a day of practicing EXQUISITE INTONATION will open your ears to a variety of tuning possibilities. It will provide you with a means of checking pitches with the vibrations of the open strings. And it will help you to develop the ability to *vary* pitches in order to provide the greatest possible musical expression. Further, the EXQUISITE INTONATION METHOD will offer you a means of improving the intonation of any piece of music you may wish to play. By practicing these scales, etudes, and excerpts, the string player of today finally will have a dependable means of playing consistently, expressively, and beautifully in tune.

2.18.76.

V.L.

Barry Ross

Part One

SYMPATHETIC VIBRATIONS

"Basically, you are either playing in tune or you are playing out of tune."

-Itzhak Perlman

SYMPATHETIC TOUCH TONES

Sympathetic vibrations from the open strings provide a means of tuning many notes precisely to the instrument. You can easily find the sympathetic tones which relate to the open strings by playing a tone that is either a unison or a partial of the overtone series of an open string.

While holding the tone, use another finger to lightly touch the related open string. When the held note is perfectly in tune, the touching will cause a little "click" sound -- the result of the sudden cutoff of the tonal support from the sympathetically vibrating open string.

Try it right now. It really works. While playing the 3rd finger *g* on the D string, touch the open G string with your 2nd finger. Do you hear the click? Be very discerning about the pitch since highly resonant notes like this G will click even if the 3rd finger *g* is slightly off center.

This procedure will verify whether or not the tone being played is in tune with the open string, as will be demonstrated by the presence or absence of sympathetic vibrations. On highly resonant notes it is sometimes possible to create this pulse at several different tunings of the same tone. In these instances it is best to choose the tuning which gives the loudest, clearest pulse.

While there are many ways of notating this procedure, this book uses diamond shaped noteheads with stems showing the rhythm of the touch. When the diamond shaped notehead indicates a particular open string to be touched, lightly TOUCH that string with the finger indicated to create the desired pulse.

Sympathetic   Touch   Tones

STALKING THOSE ELUSIVE
SYMPATHETIC VIBRATIONS

Every stringed instrument possesses its own special tone quality. That quality can often be enhanced by the addition of sympathetic vibrations from the open strings.

It is fairly simple to excite the open G, D, A, and E strings into sympathetic resonance by playing a unison or octave on another string. But one can also search farther up the overtone series for the fifth and even the major third above the fundamental open string in order to find tones which evoke similar, but more subtle, sympathetic responses from the fundamental open string.

Although some sympathetic vibrations may be impossible to uncover, the search itself can be fruitful because we know theoretically that those good little vibrations exist and because the search for them always improves our resonance and intonation.[1]

The added sound of a sympathetically vibrating open string may be as subtle as a slight shine surrounding the tone of the sustained note. Or it may be so loud and clear as to have considerable effect on the timbre and quality of the tone being produced. When the sustained note is beautifully in tune with the violin, the related open string will vibrate sympathetically.

[1]See APPENDIX for a more complete discussion of all the existing sympathetic vibrations.

SEARCHING FOR BEAUTIFUL INTONATION

Consider four factors in your search for beautiful intonation:

1. Bow Tone

If used incorrectly, the bow can have a detrimental effect upon intonation and will reduce the chances of finding sympathetic vibrations. Be certain that the interaction of bow speed, bow pressure and distance from the bridge (sounding point) is correct. Be sure to apply all of your knowledge of tone production to your work on intonation. Searching for beautiful intonation always involves playing with a resonant, free bow tone.

2. Vibrato

It is best to use little or no vibrato until after one has found the correct pitch and has activated whatever sympathetic vibrations might be available for that pitch. The addition of vibrato will then bring much greater color and richness to the tone. It will be perfectly in tune and highly resonant.

3. Adjusting Pitches Properly

In making the delicate pitch adjustments that these studies require, it is best to release the pressure of the finger on the string and replace it in a higher or lower setting without altering the finger angle. Doing this will avoid "rolling" the finger forward and backward, which can destroy the hand position and create needless tension in the left hand. In searching for sympathetic vibrations, **be sure to leave the sympathetic string free to vibrate!**

4. Ten Minutes a Day

As you spend about ten minutes a day practicing the etudes and scales in this book you should check your tuning very often. Be patient in your search for sympathetic vibrations because not all S.V.'s can be found on all instruments. Those above the third or fourth partial are very obscure.

As implied by the term "exquisite" intonation, it is the tones you have searched for and chosen that contain the beauty.

HAPPY VIBRATIONS !

THE OVERTONE SERIES

When a stretched string is bowed or plucked, it gives off not only the tone of the entire length of the string but also, in lesser strength, tones corresponding to halves, thirds, quarters, fifths, etc. of the entire length. These are called partials, or harmonics.

Just as the mixing of various primary colors on a pallet creates varying hues, the partials of a vibrating open string create the quality and timbre of the string tone, as differentiated from the tone of, say, a clarinet. If we take the open G as the fundamental tone, the series of tones produced in this way will be, in ascending pitch, G G D G B D F G A B, etc., representing the proportional divisions.[1]

The set of tones and intervals derived in this fashion is called the "overtone series". The tones or partials of the series bear fundamental relationships to one another and are often used on stringed instruments to produce natural harmonics. **Sympathetic vibrations can occur on an open string whenever any note belonging to that string's overtone series is played.**

[1] "Intonation and Musical Meaning," Walter Piston, C. Bruno & Son, 1963

Overtone Series

Sympathetic Vibrations

Touching with Third Finger Sustained

Barry Ros

1) Tune violin carefully. 2) Gently touch the diamond shaped open string as indicated. 3) Adjust the sustained tone to provide maximum sympathetic resonance on the "touching" string.

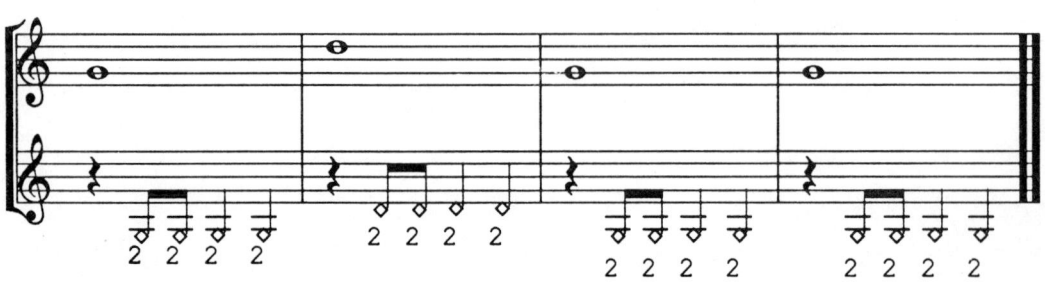

Sympathetic Vibrations

Touching with 4th Finger Sustained

Barry Ross

1) Tune violin carefully. 2) Gently touch the diamond shaped open string as indicated. 3) Adjust the sustained tone to provide maximum sympathetic resonance on the "touching" string.

15

ETUDE

Barry Ross

1) Tune Violin Carefully; 2) Gently touch the diamond shaped open string with the finger indicated.

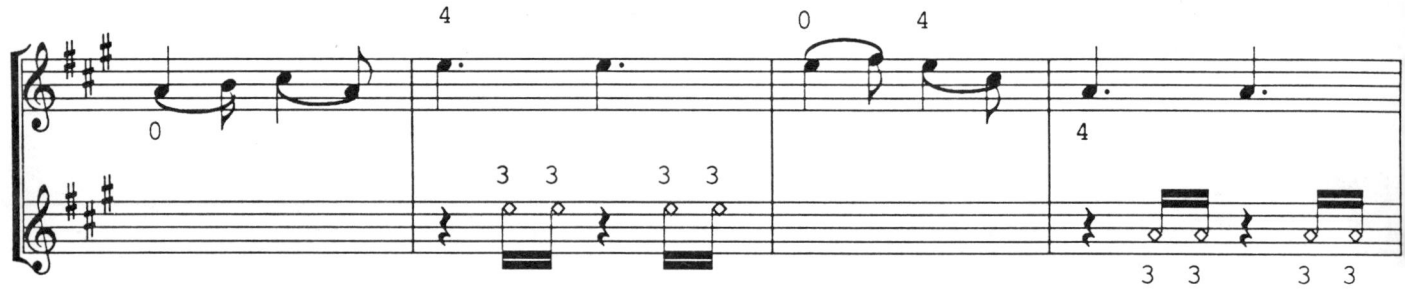

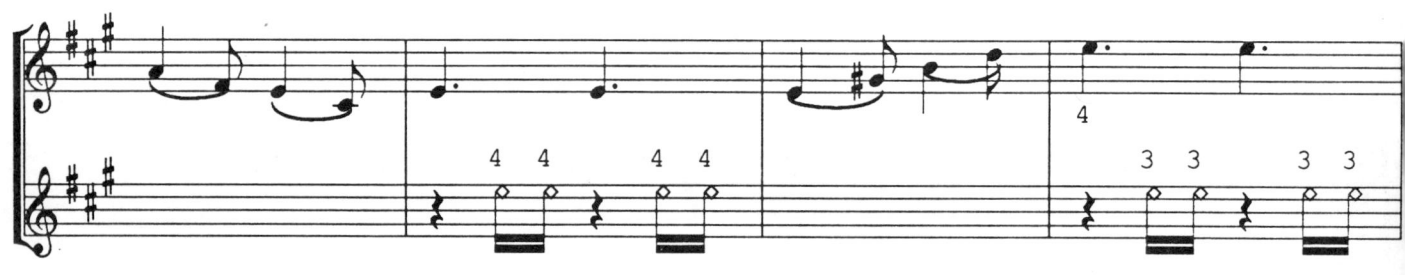

17

Etude

Barry Ross

1) Tune violin carefully. 2) Gently touch the diamond shaped open string as indicated. 3) Adjust the sustained tone to provide maximum sympathetic resonance on the "touching" string.

18

Part Two

MELODIC INTONATION

MELODIC INTONATION

One of the great advantages and pleasures of playing a stringed instrument is the ability of the player to adjust tones expressively. Playing in tune means playing each pitch in accordance with its musical function, be it harmonic or melodic. It is this ability to vary pitches functionally -- thus providing great depth and variety of color -- that makes stringed instruments so very gratifying for both the player and the listener.

In playing a C major scale starting on middle *c*, notice how the leading tone function of the *e* natural on the D string invites a <u>high</u> tuning for that note.

This *e* natural, which will elicit a strong sympathetic response from the open E, and which, if played in first position, is well in tune with the open A string, functions as a leading tone upward. Possessing as it does a strong magnetism upward toward the subdominant *f*, it is much higher than the *e* natural one might play in a D major scale.

The <u>low</u> *e* natural which sounds appropriate for the D major scale is well in tune with the open G string and sounds too flat in a C major scale. *E* natural in the key of D major has no upward melodic magnetism and, therefore, relates more to the D tonic and its subdominant, the open G string. This tuning brings no sympathetic response from the open E.

In major scales, the 3rd and 7th steps (*e* and *b* in C major) often function as leading tones upward and tend toward a higher "melodic" tuning. Similarly, the tonic (*c*) and subdominant (*f*) often function as leading tones downward and tend toward the *b* and *e*. In minor scales, the sixth degree is often played low, close to the fifth. **From this example it is clear that the pitch of any written note can vary from key to key depending upon the leading tone function of the note.** One major purpose of this book is to teach the essential ability to play the same written note at different pitches.

Play the following two scales beautifully in tune by following the plus (+) designations for tones that function as leading tones higher and the minus (-) designations for tones that lead lower. In the C major scale, notice the raised *e* and *b* . In the D major scale, notice the raised *f#* and *c#* and the lowered *e* and *b*, which had been raised in the previous scale. Begin to hear how these MELODIC leading tones function differently in the two scales. Use the printed open string double stops to check your tuning.

Two Melodic Scales

C Major

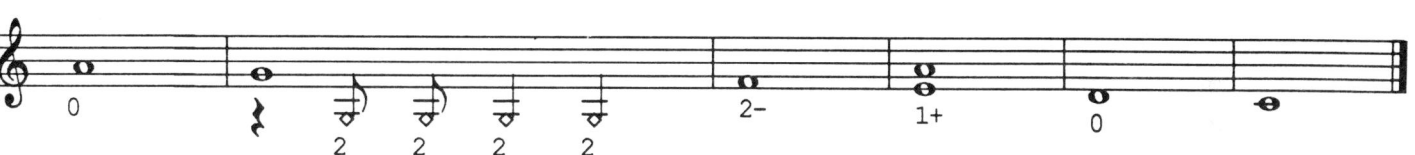

D Major

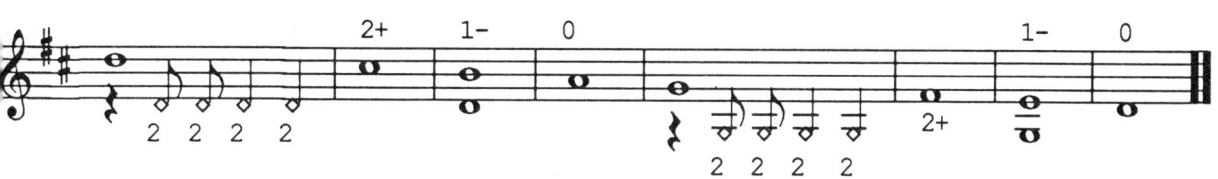

Chromatic Melodic Scale

Barry Ross

1) Take as many bows as necessary on each note. 2) Exaggerate the high (+) and low (-) indications. 3) Touch the open strings for maximum sympathetic vibrations.

23

Bach Allemanda Exercise

Bach

1) "Touch" for all sympathetic vibrations. Then establish the proper tuning for each note by adjusting the tones either higher (+) or lower (-) as indicated.

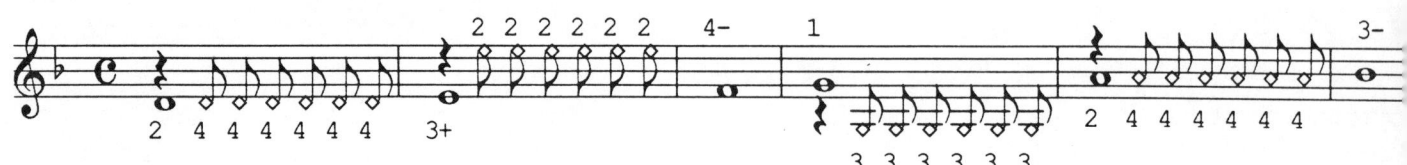

24

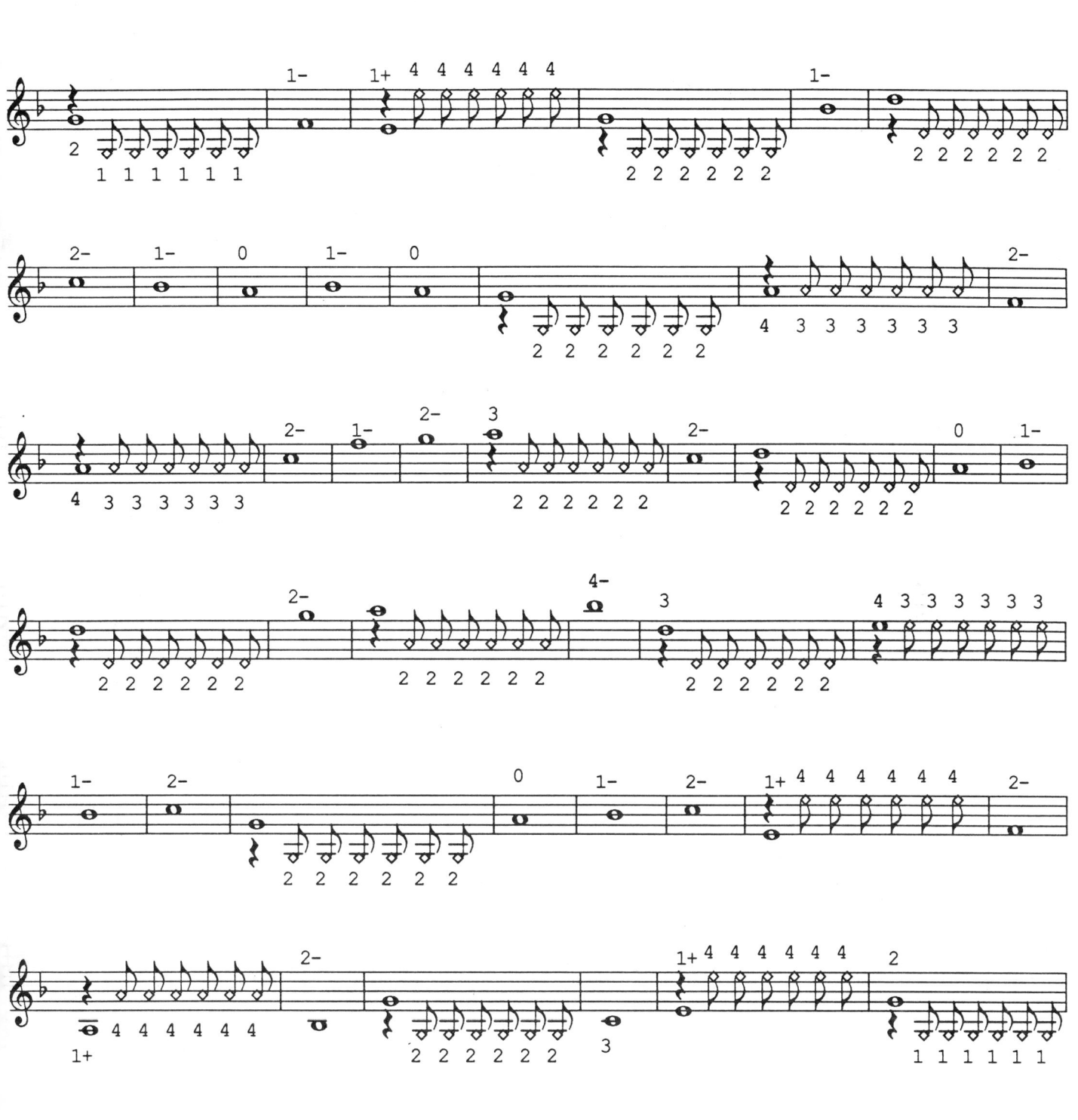

25

Allemanda

Bach

Play through the opening of the
Allemanda slowly using the low (-) and
high (+) tunings you have just practiced.
Continue to check for sympathetic
vibrations. Enjoy the beauty of your
exquisite intonation.

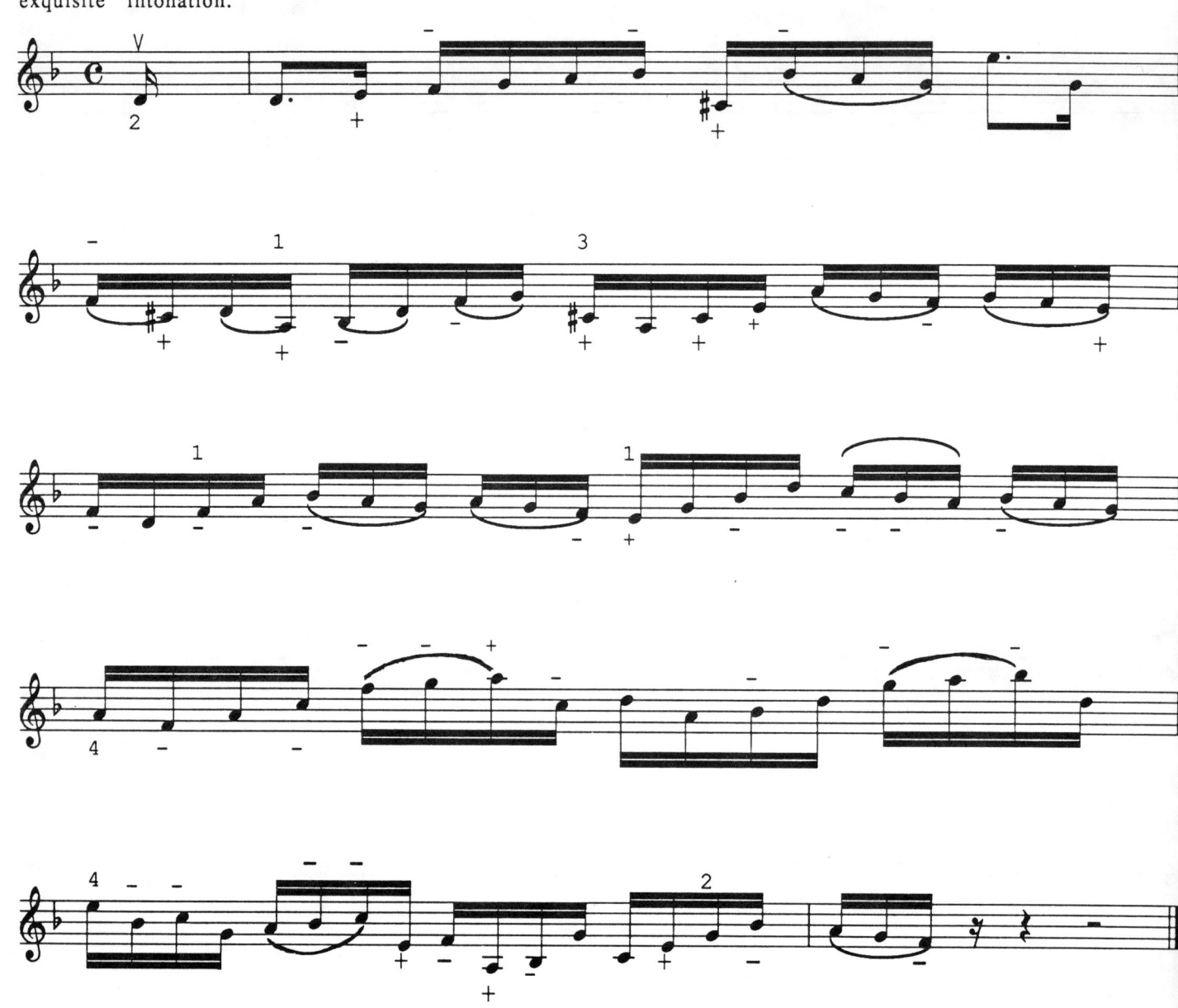

26

Part Three

HARMONIC INTONATION

HARMONIC INTONATION

Music that involves considerable double stop playing, such as the *Bach Unaccompanied Sonatas and Partitas*, often requires that chords and double stops be tuned in accordance with certain harmonic principles. Accompanying voices in string quartets must often adjust pitches to this HARMONIC tuning when the harmonic function needs to predominate. *When more than one voice is sounding, the string player must decide whether it is more appropriate to use combination tone tuning rather than melodic tuning in order to arrive at the desired intonation.*

The following scales contrast MELODIC tuning with HARMONIC tuning. Notice in HARMONIC tuning how <u>high</u> you must make the second finger in order to play it in tune with the next higher string. Notice also how <u>high</u> the flatted first finger must be played in order for it to be in tune with the adjacent lower string. Listen carefully to hear the differences between the two scales.

Explore these two types of tunings, MELODIC and HARMONIC, in order to be able to make these subtle adjustments whenever you wish.

Two Chromatic Scales on G

The first scale involves using MELODIC intonation; the second uses HARMONIC intonation. Practice both scales until you can clearly hear the differences.

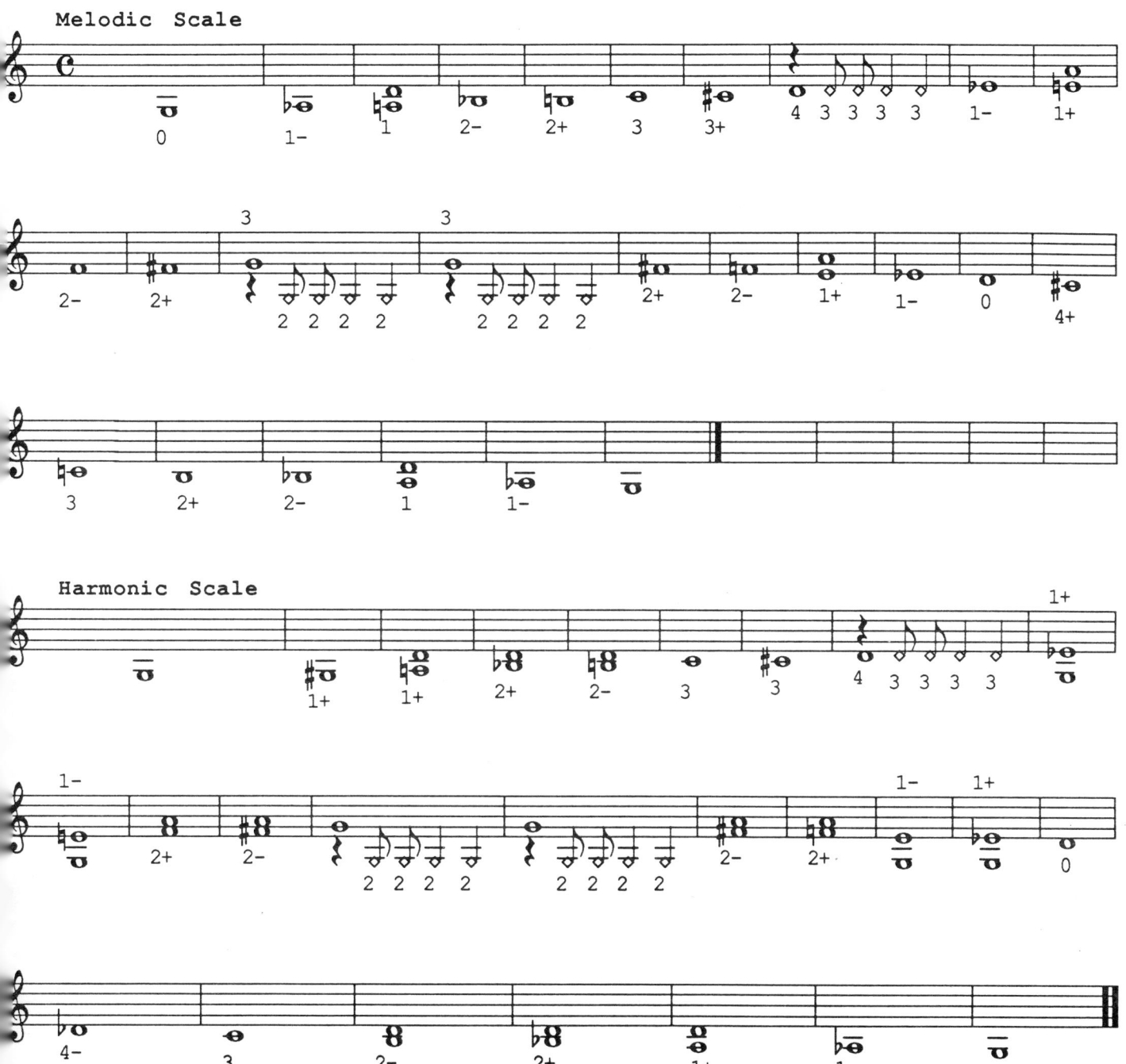

29

Two Chromatic Scales on D

The first scale involves using MELODIC intonation; the second uses HARMONIC intonation. Practice both scales until you can clearly hear the differences.

Melodic Scale

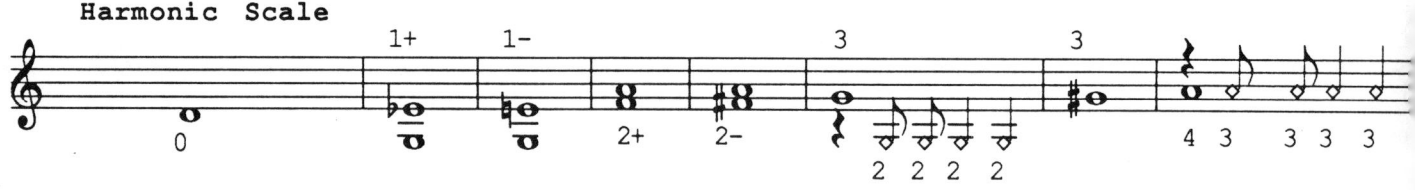

Harmonic Scale

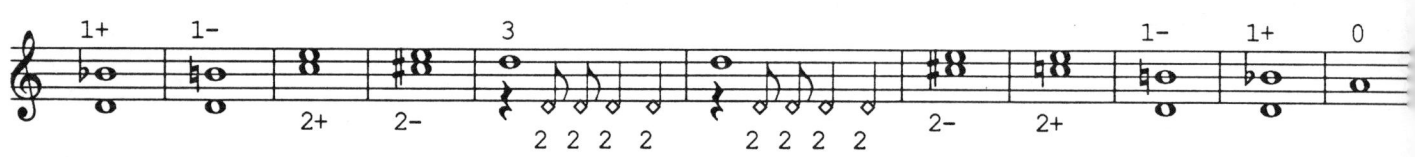

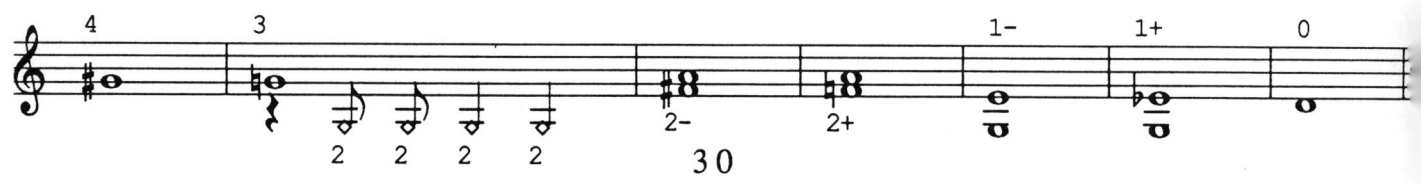

Two Chromatic Scales on A

e first scale involves using MELODIC
onation; the second uses HARMONIC
onation. Practice both scales until you
n clearly hear the difference.

Two Chromatic Scales on E

The first scale involves using MELODIC intonation; the second uses HARMONIC intonation. Practice both scales until you can clearly hear the differences.

Part Four

COMBINATION TONES

STALKING THOSE ELUSIVE
COMBINATION TONES

Until now we have explored overtones and sympathetic vibrations found in a melodic, single note context. Another equally important and quite separate phenomenon governs intonation when two or more tones are sounded simultaneously.

Paul Hindemith[1] has written that when a stringed instrument plays a double stop, additional tones are produced which are called "combination tones." They are usually so weak that the superficial ear does not perceive them. They are, however, of great importance to the subconscious ear because they bear a mathematical relationship to the two directly produced tones, serving to define these tones harmonically. The string player hears them as soft bass tones when playing double stops. Once the ear has become aware of them, it hears them easily.

The existence of combination tones provides a point of reference by which the directly produced tones can be evaluated for their purity of intonation. When the two directly produced tones are consonant with the combination tone, the resulting intonation is pure and harmonious. As with sympathetic vibrations, exquisitely tuned combination tones can greatly enhance the resonance of your tone.

It is important to clearly understand the difference between overtones and combination tones.

Overtones are produced in varying number by a single sounding tone and resonate to the perfect tuning of the open strings. Combination tones arise only when two or more tones are sounded simultaneously. *Both overtones and combination tones have a profound effect upon intonation.*

The sounding of combination tones produces additional but less intense combination tones, thus creating several orders of tones. It is only the first two orders which are sufficiently prominent to be heard.

[1] Paul Hindemith: THE CRAFT OF MUSICAL COMPOSITION, Chapter 2, Copyright 1945, Associated Music Publishers, Inc., New York.

COMBINATION TONE CHART

Interval	First Order				Second Order			
Unison:	Unison				Unison			
Minor 3rd:	2 Oct. & M3	Below Bottom Note			M3	Below Bottom Note		
Major 3rd:	2 Oct.	"	"	"	P4	"	"	"
Perfect 4th:	1 Oct.&P5	"	"	"	P5	"	"	"
Perfect 5th:	1 Oct.	"	"	"	1 Oct.	"	"	"
Minor 6th:	M 6	"	"	"	Oct & M3	"	"	"
Major 6th:	P 5	"	"	"	Oct. & P5	"	"	"
Octave:	Unison				Unison			

Combination Tone Table

Gerald Fischbach

Directly Produced Pitches ○
Combination Tones of the First Order ◆
Combination Tones of the Second Order ◇

Combination Tones on Thirds

Barry Ross

1) Practice these intervals as written, then starting on the D and G strings. 2) Hold each chord as long as necessary to precisely tune the combination tones in the bass clef.

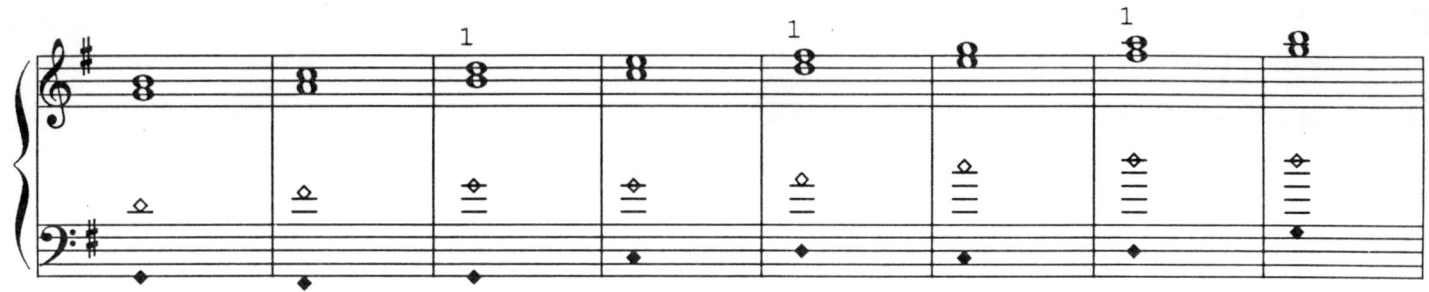

36

Combination Tones on Sixths

Barry Ross

1) Practice these intervals as written, then starting on the D and G strings. 2) Hold each chord as long as necessary to precisely tune the combination tones in the bass clef.

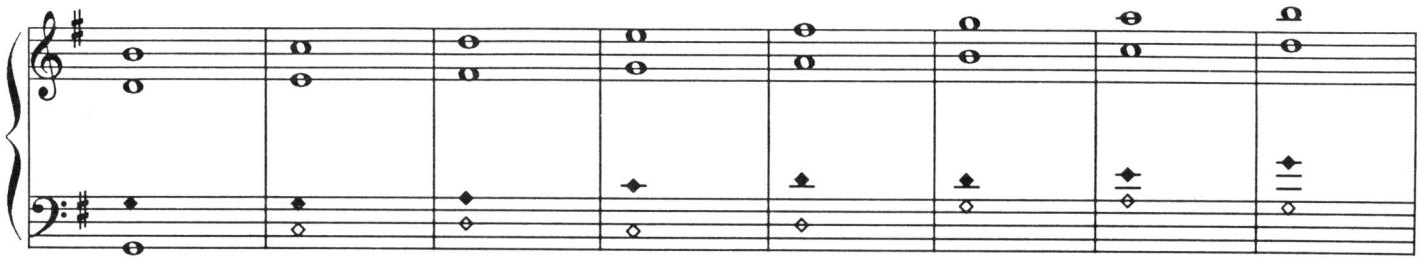

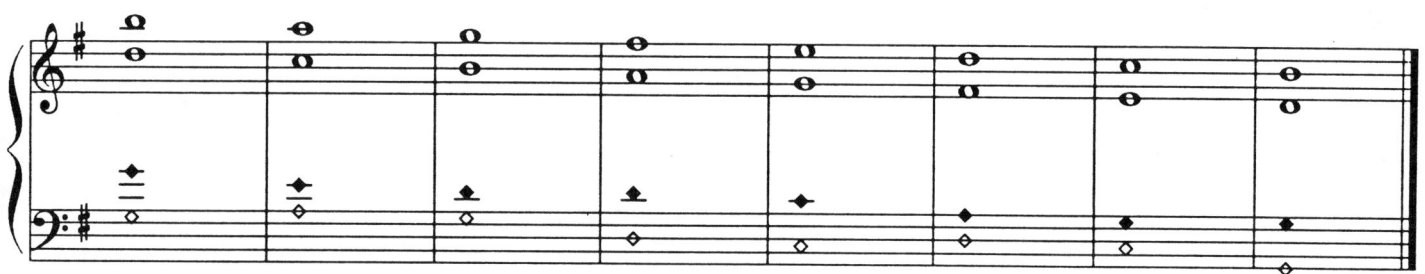

37

Open String Combination Tone Scale

Sustain each double stop until the combination tones are perfectly in tune with the directly produced tones.

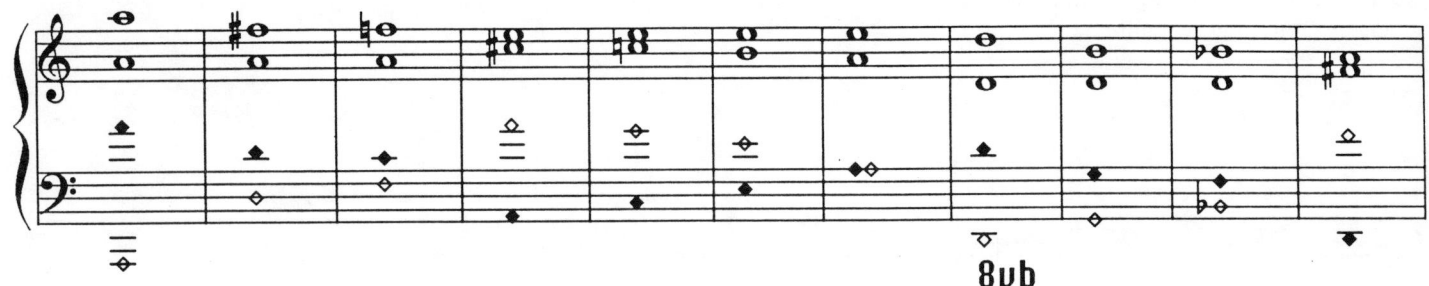

8υb

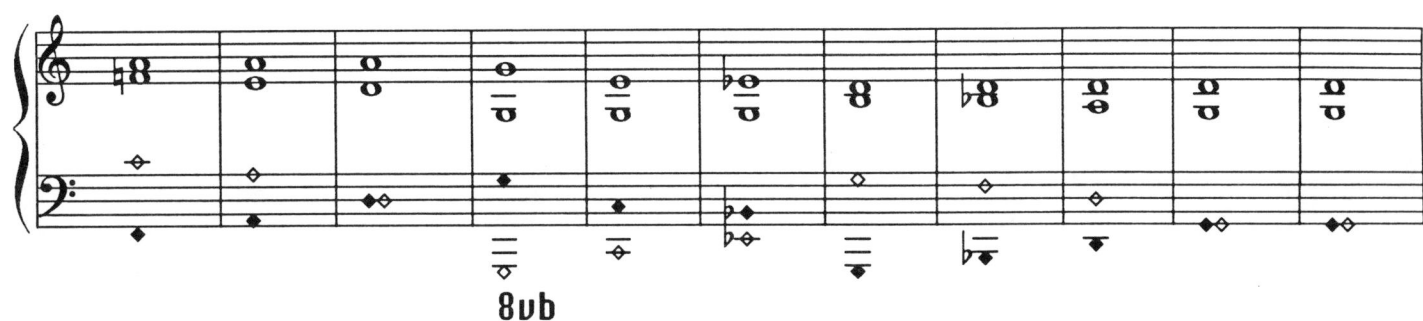

8υb

8υb

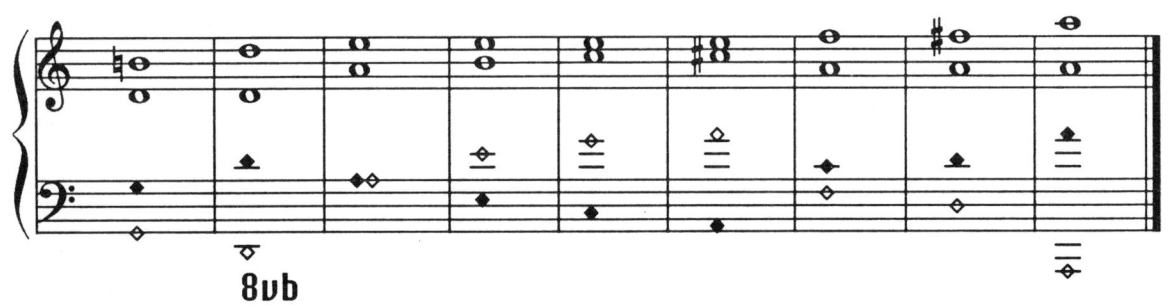

8υb

38

Ciaccona Combination Tones

Sustain and tune each chord until you can
clearly hear the combination tones
shown in the bass clef below.

Harmonic Intonation #1

Barry Ross

1) Tune violin carefully. 2) Adjust the pitches of the fingered note as indicated until it sounds perfectly in tune with the open string.

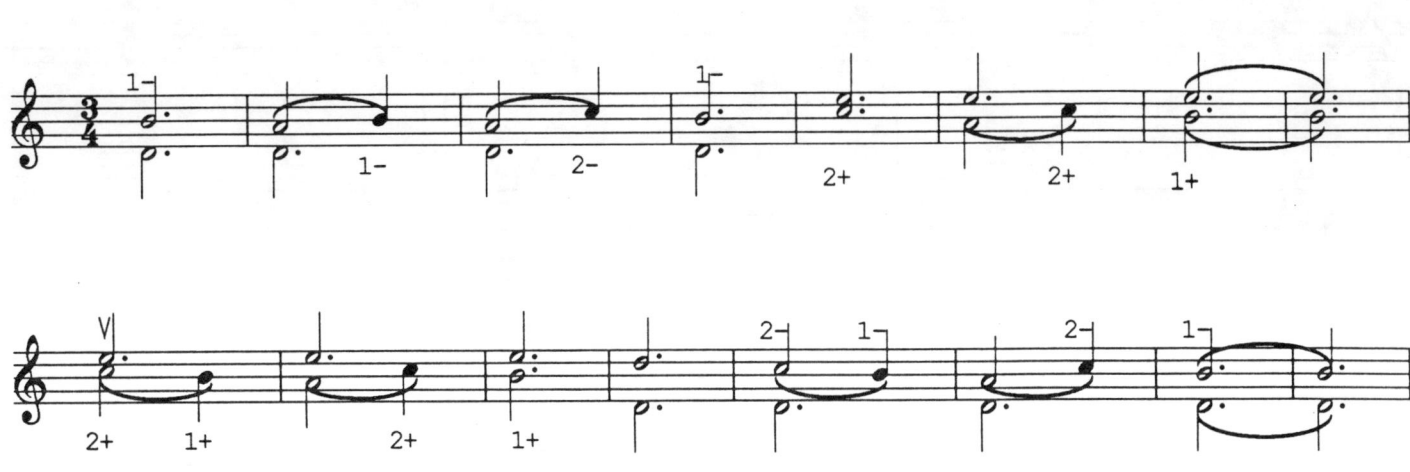

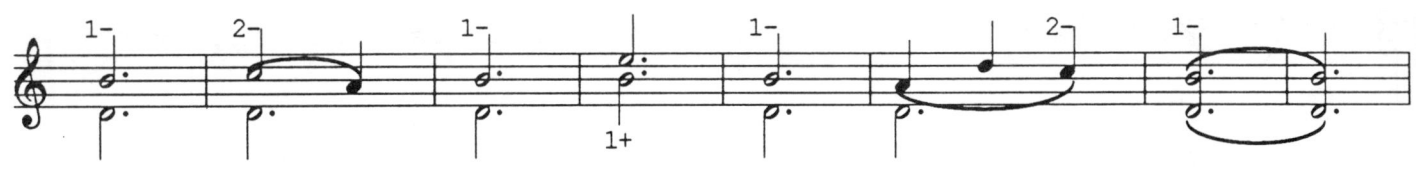

Harmonic Intonation #2

Barry Ross

1) Tune violin carefully. 2) Adjust each fingered note to the open string. 3) Notice how high the first and second fingers must be played in order to be in tune with the open strings.

41

EXQUISITE TUNING FOR
ALMOST EVERY NOTE

Most notes on the violin have at least two possible tunings. **It is the performer's responsibility to carefully select either the high or the low tuning,** depending upon the melodic or harmonic context.

SYMPATHETIC VIBRATIONS and COMBINATION TONES provide two separate but related means of establishing intonation anchors for all but a handful of "lost" notes. The placement of lost tones is determined by their relationship to neighboring tones.

The following examples detail those notes which can be related to sympathetic vibrations (Sympathetic Tones), those that can be tuned to open strings (Open String Combination Tones), and those that do not relate to any specific natural reference point on the violin ("Lost" Tones).

Sympathetic   Tones

Open String Combination Tones

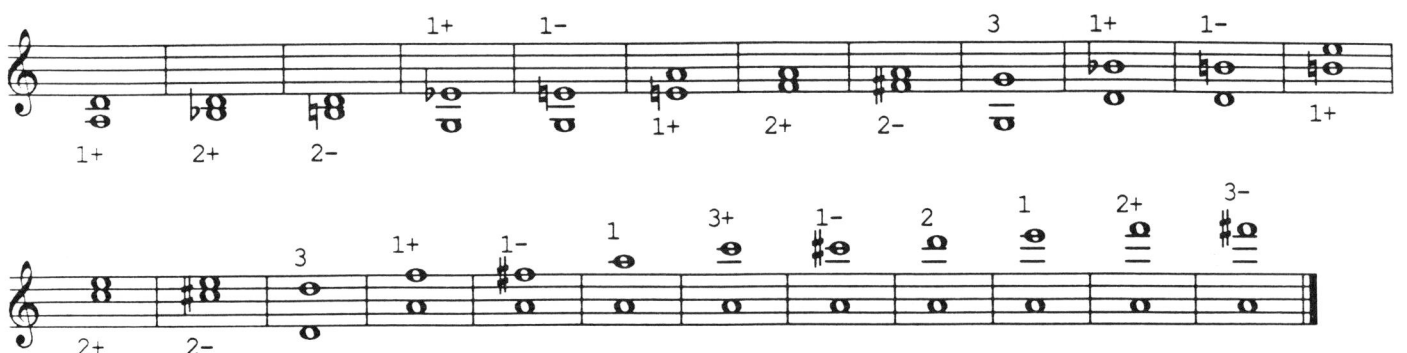

"Lost" Tones

Pitch Determined by Relationship to Other Tones

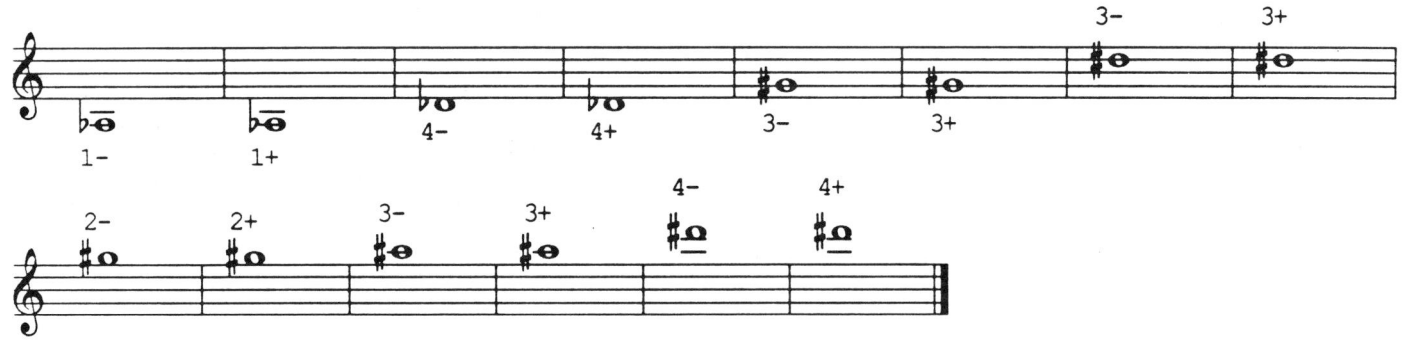

Comprehensive Scale on G

Barry Ross

This scale provides 2 tunings for most notes. 1) Adjust the notes higher (+) or lower (-) where indicated. 2) Tune double stops to the open strings. 3) Touch for sympathetic vibrations where indicated.

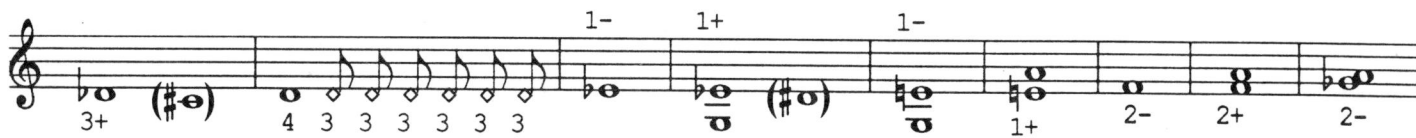

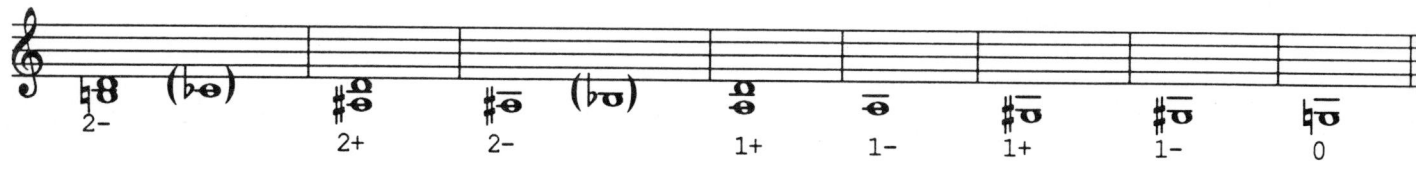

Comprehensive Scale on A

Barry Ross

This scale provides 2 tunings for most notes. 1) Adjust the notes higher (+) or lower (-) where indicated. 2) Tune double stops to the open strings. 3) Touch for sympathetic vibrations where indicated.

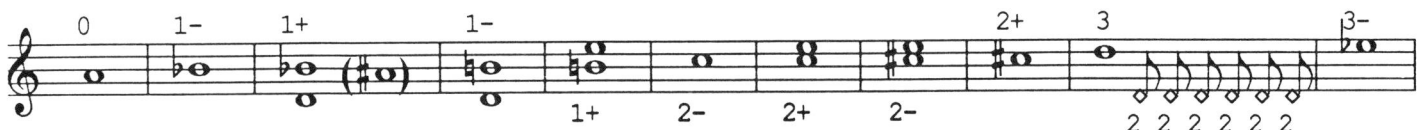

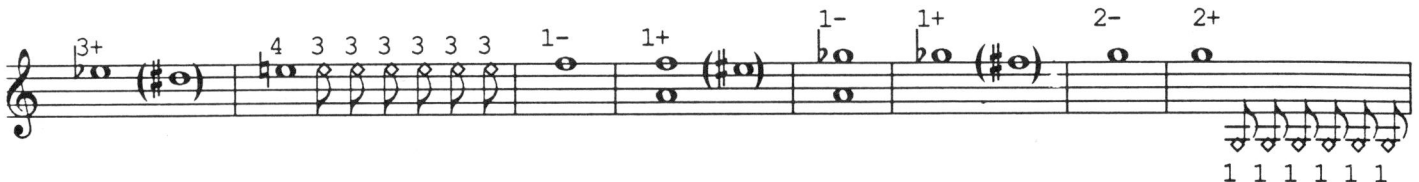

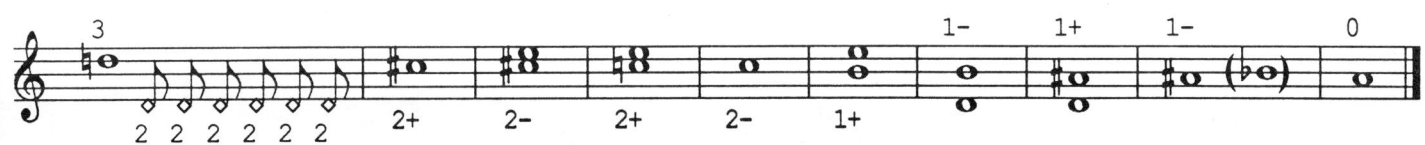

The Guarneri String Quartet
Arnold Steinhardt and John Dalley, Violins,
Michael Tree, Viola, and David Soyer, Cello

Part Five

EXCERPTS

Yo-Yo Ma, Cello and Samuel Sanders, Piano

THE EXQUISITE INTONATION
METHOD

1) **Tune violin carefully.**
   Start with a good "A" from the piano, or a dependable electronic source. Listen for the combination tones of the open strings.

2) **Make all the notes of a given passage LONG; use a resonant bow sound that will encourage the free vibrations of the string.**
   This is an important rule, for it will allow you to take notes OUT OF RHYTHM and adjust them for ideal pitch. As you improve the pitches, the <u>resonance</u> will also be enhanced.

3) **As you play the notes, touch the open strings for all possible sympathetic vibrations.**
   You should be able to verify the pitches of many notes simply by touching the open strings for the sympathetic vibrations.

4) **On all notes, determine whether you wish to use HIGH (+) or LOW (-) tuning.**
   As you practice the passage out of rhythm, experiment with the tunings to determine which you prefer. Decide whether or not the note functions HARMONICALLY or MELODICALLY. Select your preferred tuning for <u>every</u> note of the passage.

5) **Practice the tunings that you have chosen, especially those tunings to which you are unaccustomed.**
   The ear tends to become accustomed to whatever intonation you happen to be playing. BE MISTRUSTFUL OF YOUR INTONATION! Question each note until you are satisfied that it is exactly where it belongs. **<u>Your tone will gain artistic maturity.</u>**

6) **Now play the passage in rhythm, making certain to keep the pitches that you have chosen.**
   As you return to the rhythm and tempo of the passage, check to be sure that you have not altered the tuning you established when all the notes were long.

7) **Finally, add vibrato, dynamics, and expression.**
   Your ear should now be <u>convinced</u> of the pitches you have selected. The addition of vibrato, dynamics, and expression will bring the passage into a complete musical expression. Notice, too, how your improved intonation and resonance have made the passage sound more expressive.

Kreutzer Number 2 Exercise

This famous etude can be played with at least two possible tunings. Practice both tuning "A" and tuning "B". Then decide which you prefer.

A. Melodic

B. Harmonic

51

Kreutzer, Number 2

Play this etude slowly, using whichever tunings you established in the preceding exercize.

A. Melodic Finger Placement

B. Harmonic Finger Placement

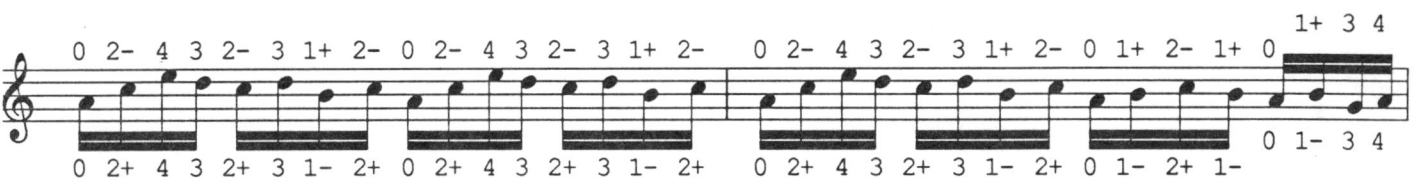

Concerto No. 5 in A

Mozart

Beethoven Romance Exercise

Barry Ross

Beethoven's Romance can be played with
many possible tunings. Practice both A
and B finger placements. Then decide
which you prefer for each note. The lower
staff refers to "A", Melodic tunings.

A. Melodic

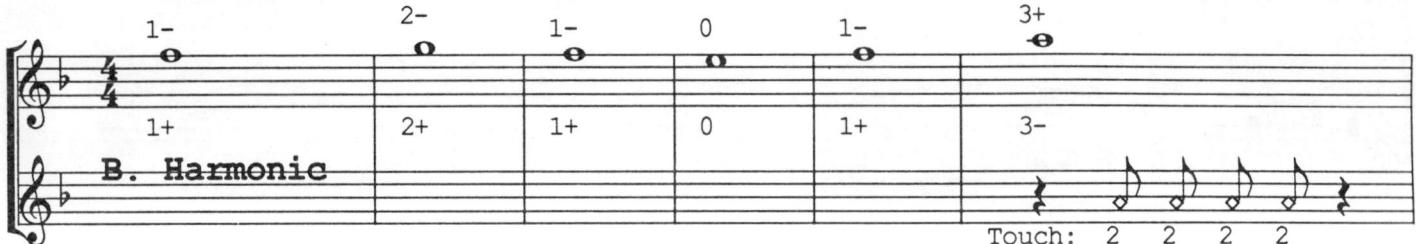

B. Harmonic

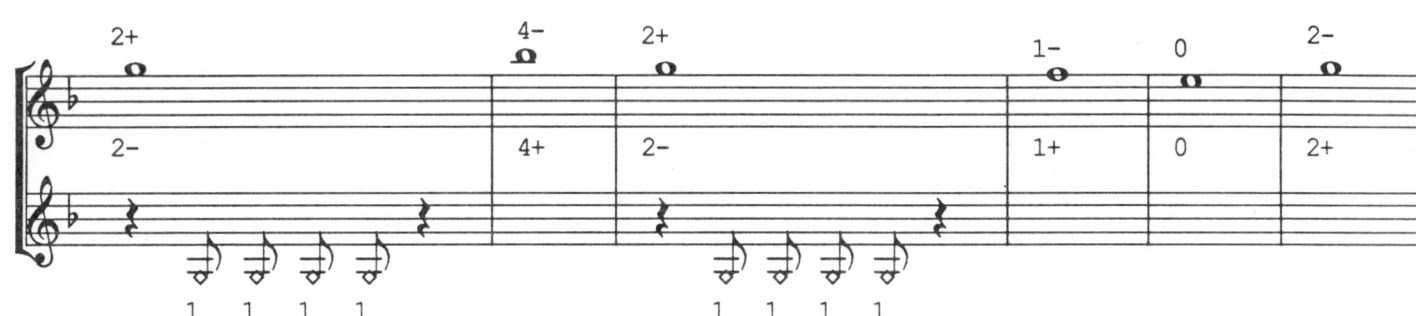

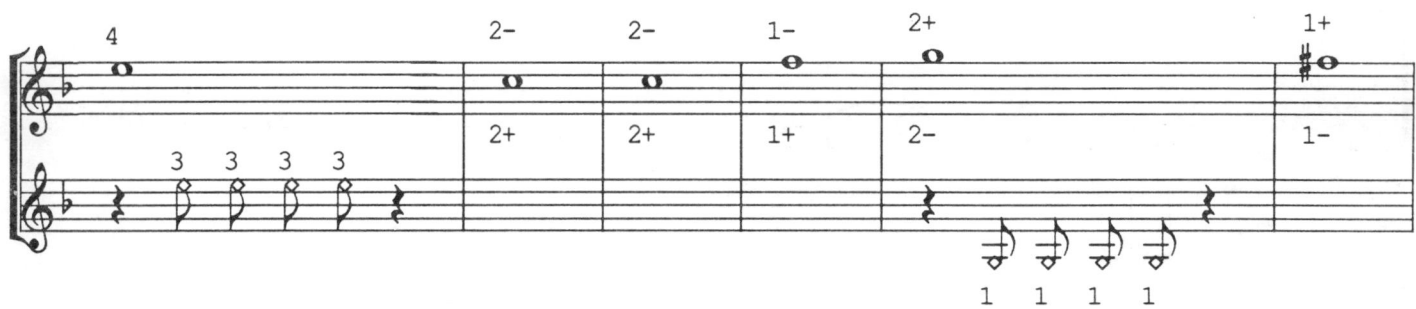

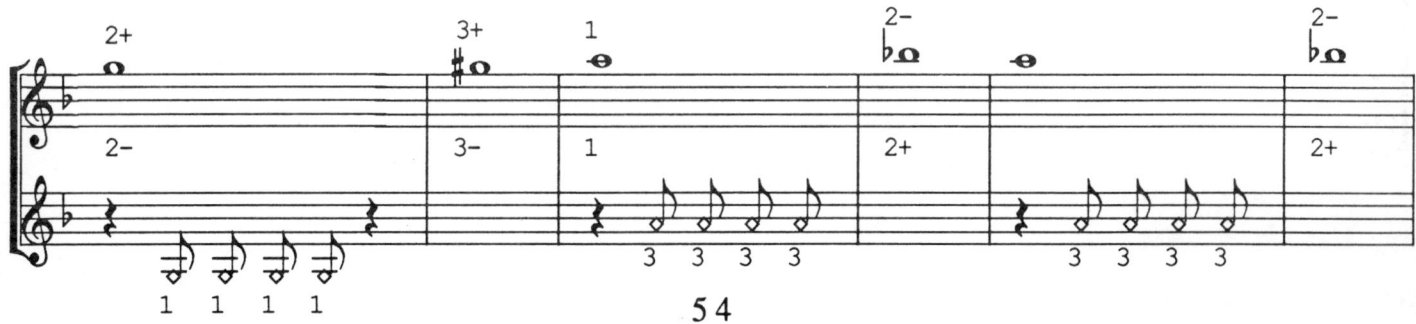

54

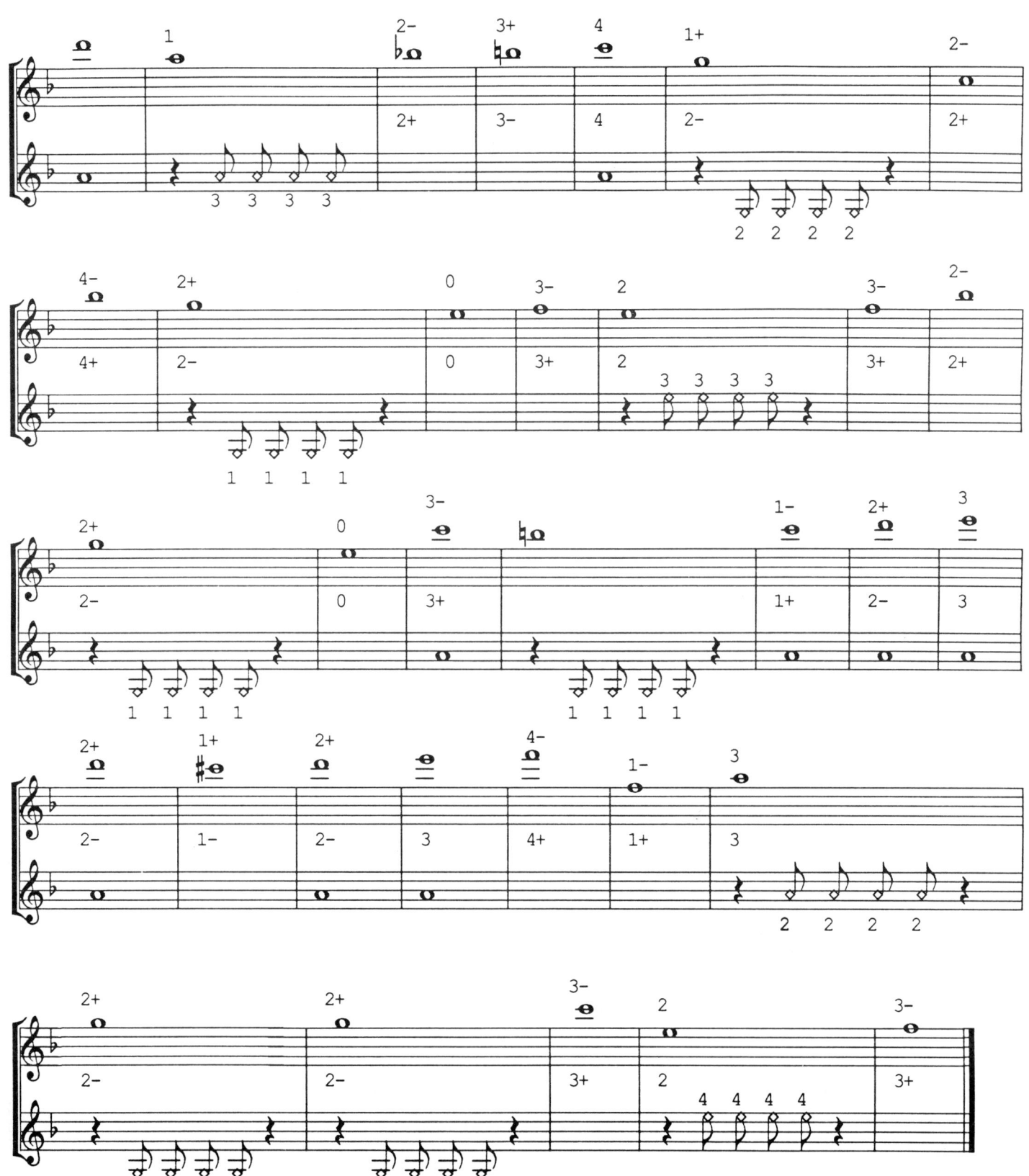

Now that you have established the pitches with which you will be working, play the *Beethoven Romance* excerpt slowly in rhythm, being careful not to fall back into your natural intonation. Try to keep the same perfection of intonation and resonance while playing the passage in rhythm. During long notes it is still possible to check for sympathetic vibrations by touching the open strings.

Romance in F

Beethoven

Because of the power of the vibrations of E natural, notice how out of tune the first note, F, sounds when played as a 1+. The leading tone, E, encourages the use of a low F (1-) in this context.

Adagio cantabile

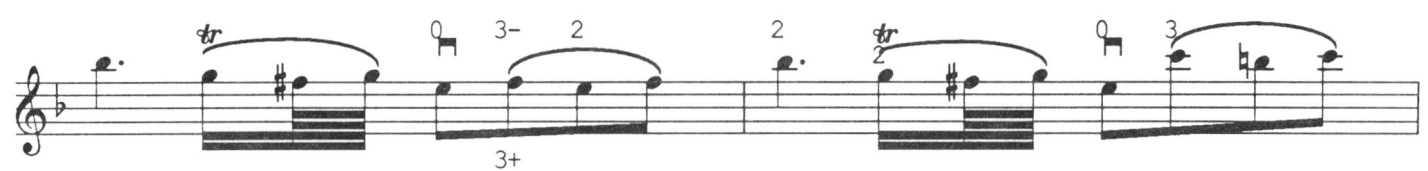

Opus 132 Exercise

BEETHOVEN

In this excerpt, the C# could be played
high (melodically) or low (harmonically).
Choose one or the other for each C#.

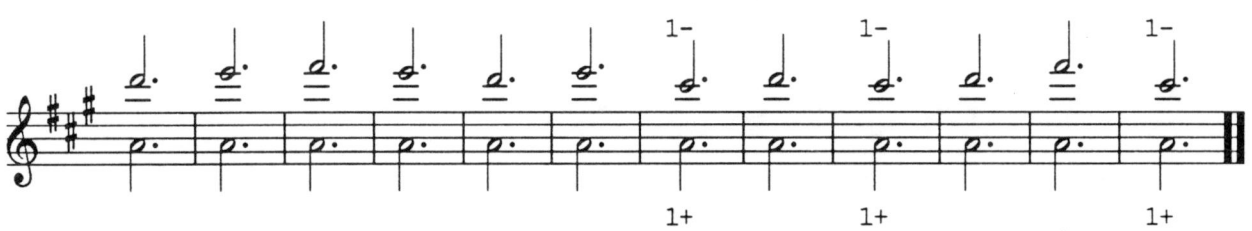

Beethoven, Opus 132

Now incorporate the tunings you have just chosen into this original version of Beethoven, opus 132.

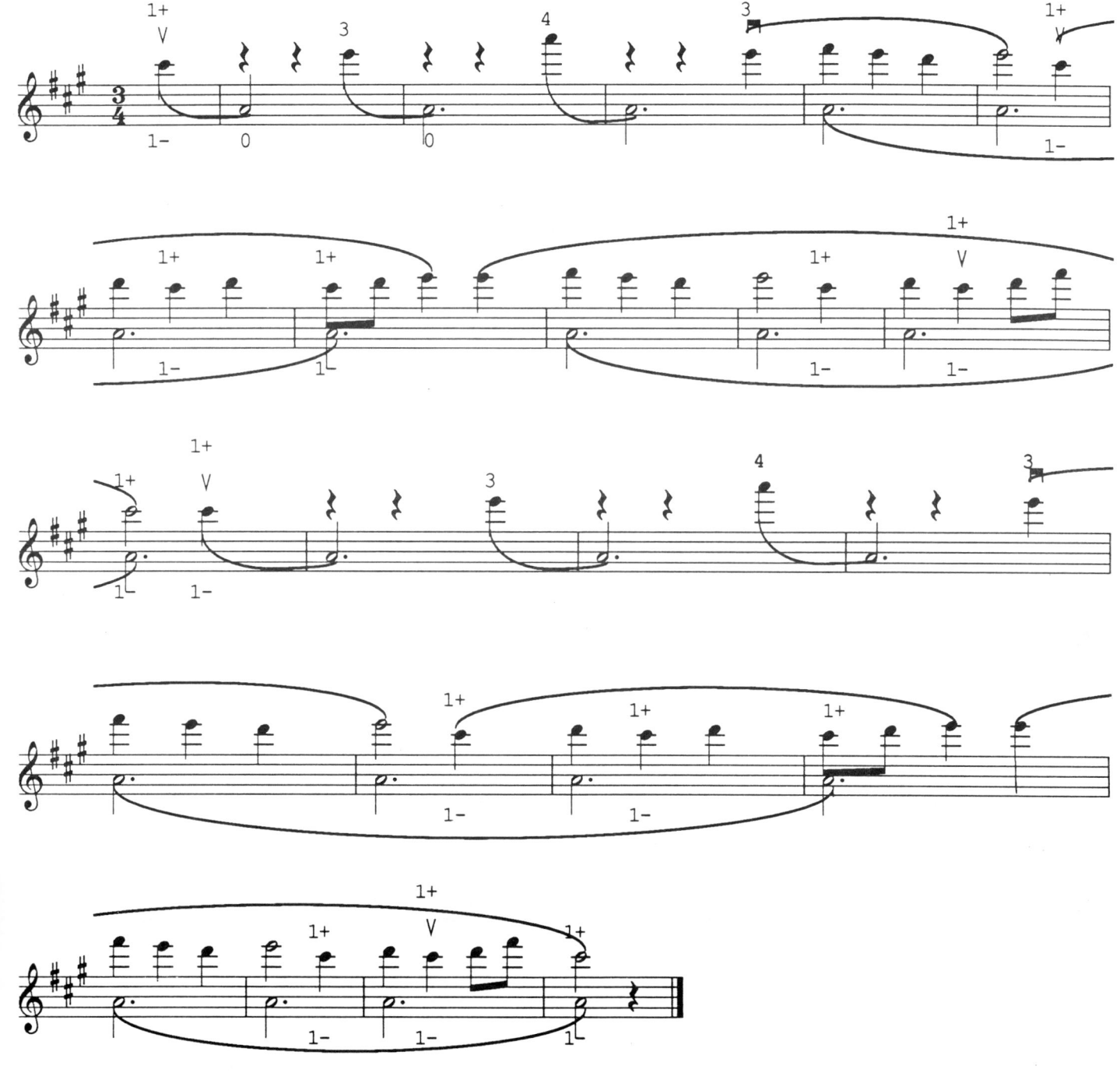

Ciaccona

Bach

1) Tune Violin Carefully. 2) Play the exercise slowly listening carefully to the harmonies. 3) Decide whether or not to use the melodic leading tones as indicated.

D MAJOR: F#+   **A MAJOR: C#+**

E MAJOR: G#+   **A MAJOR: C#+**

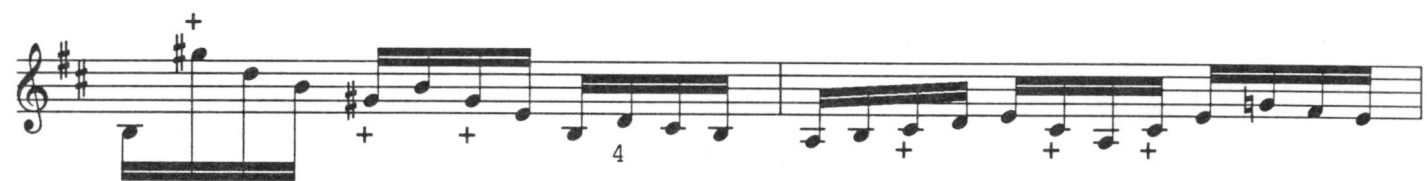

D MAJOR: F#+   **A MAJOR: C#+**

B MINOR: D-   **A MAJOR: C#+**

D MAJOR: F#+   **A MAJOR:C#+**

B MINOR: D-   **A MAJOR: C#+**

D MAJOR: F#+   **A MAJOR: C#+**

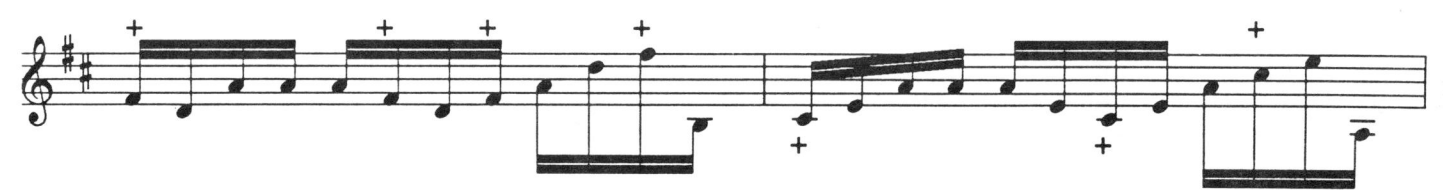

E7: G#+   **A7: C#+,**   **G-**   **D MAJOR**

APPENDIX

Although they are often elusive, sympathetic vibrations <u>theoretically</u> exist on the fundamental open G with any *g, d,* or *b* not on the G string; on the open D with any *d, a,* or *f#* not on the D string; on the open A with any *a, e,* or *c#* not on the A string; and on the open E with any *e, b,* or *g#* not on the E string.

As one seeks sympathetic vibrations higher in the overtone series, the sympathetic resonances become more obscure. Although most instruments are not sensitive enough to produce the higher overtones of the open strings, certain unexpected ones can sometimes be found:

1.   *B* **on the E string** has a strong effect on resonating the **open G**, even though it is fairly high in the overtone series.

2.   The **high *b* on the A string** excites the **open E** into clear vibrations, but the high *e* on the D string does not have as dramatic an effect upon the open A, nor does the high *a* on the G string strongly affect the open D. All of these notes have similar relationships in the overtone series. It may be that, because the high *e* on the D string and the high *a* on the G string resonate their own open strings, their effect upon the strings to which their relationship is more distant may be diminished.

3.   **High *g* on the E string** will give only a very faint resonance to the **open G** string, probably because of its three octave distance up the overtone series.

4.   **D on the E string** seems to have a stronger effect resonating the **open A** than the **open D** on some violins. This suggests that the system can work backwards as well, using the open A as a partial of the high *d*. Here again, however, the corresponding relationships of the *g* **on the A string** and the *c* **on the D string** do not significantly excite the open D and G respectively.

Copy editing & type design
by
Barbara J. Ross
MacRoss·Words
18 Bradford Road
Hingham, MA 02043